HAL•LEONARD®

VIOLIN PLAY-ALONG

AUDIO ACCESS INCLUDED

Songs *for* BEGINNERS

CONTENTS

To access audio visit:
www.halleonard.com/mylibrary

Enter Code
4262-2748-0476-1962

ISBN 978-1-4803-9839-9

HAL•LEONARD®
CORPORATION
7777 W. BLUEMOUND RD. P.O. BOX 13819 MILWAUKEE, WI 53213

In Australia Contact:
Hal Leonard Australia Pty. Ltd.
4 Lentara Court
Cheltenham, Victoria, 3192 Australia
Email: ausadmin@halleonard.com.au

Jerry Loughney, violin
Recorded and produced by Dan Maske

Visit Hal Leonard Online at
www.halleonard.com

Amazing Grace

Words by John Newton
Traditional American Melody

America, the Beautiful

Words by Katharine Lee Bates
Music by Samuel A. Ward

Aura Lee

Words by W.W. Fosdick
Music by George R. Poulton

Ode to Joy

By Ludwig van Beethoven

Can Can

from ORPHEUS IN THE UNDERWORLD
By Jacques Offenbach

The Surprise Symphony

By Franz Joseph Haydn

This Old Man
Traditional

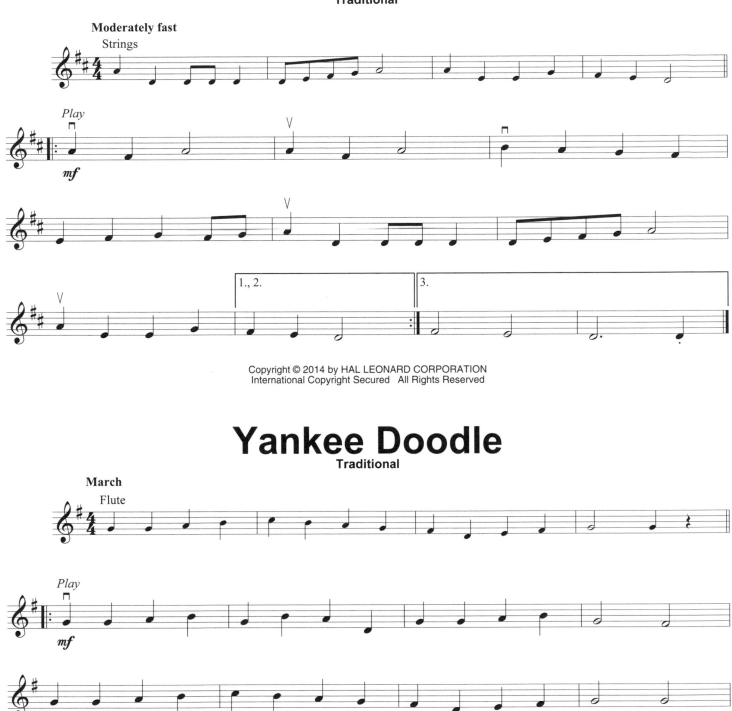

Yankee Doodle
Traditional

The Violin Play-Along Series

Play your favorite songs quickly and easily!

Just follow the music, listen to the CD or online audio to hear how the violin should sound, and then play along using the separate backing tracks. The audio files are enhanced so you can adjust the recordings to any tempo without changing pitch!

1. Bluegrass
00842152 Book/CD Pack $14.99

2. Popular Songs
00842153 Book/CD Pack $14.99

3. Classical
00842154 Book/CD Pack $14.99

4. Celtic
00842155 Book/CD Pack $14.99

5. Christmas Carols
00842156 Book/CD Pack $14.99

6. Holiday Hits
00842157 Book/CD Pack $14.99

7. Jazz
00842196 Book/CD Pack $14.99

8. Country Classics
00842230 Book/CD Pack $12.99

9. Country Hits
00842231 Book/CD Pack $14.99

10. Bluegrass Favorites
00842232 Book/CD Pack $14.99

11. Bluegrass Classics
00842233 Book/CD Pack $14.99

12. Wedding Classics
00842324 Book/CD Pack $14.99

13. Wedding Favorites
00842325 Book/CD Pack $14.99

14. Blues Classics
00842427 Book/CD Pack $14.99

15. Stephane Grappelli
00842428 Book/CD Pack $14.99

16. Folk Songs
00842429 Book/CD Pack $14.99

17. Christmas Favorites
00842478 Book/CD Pack $14.99

18. Fiddle Hymns
00842499 Book/CD Pack $14.99

19. Lennon & McCartney
00842564 Book/CD Pack $14.99

20. Irish Tunes
00842565 Book/CD Pack $14.99

21. Andrew Lloyd Webber
00842566 Book/CD Pack $14.99

22. Broadway Hits
00842567 Book/CD Pack $14.99

23. Pirates of the Caribbean
00842625 Book/CD Pack $14.99

24. Rock Classics
00842640 Book/CD Pack $14.99

25. Classical Masterpieces
00842642 Book/CD Pack $14.99

26. Elementary Classics
00842643 Book/CD Pack $14.99

27. Classical Favorites
00842646 Book/CD Pack $14.99

28. Classical Treasures
00842647 Book/CD Pack $14.99

29. Disney Favorites
00842648 Book/CD Pack $14.99

30. Disney Hits
00842649 Book/CD Pack $14.99

31. Movie Themes
00842706 Book/CD Pack $14.99

32. Favorite Christmas Songs
00102110 Book/CD Pack $14.99

33. Hoedown
00102161 Book/CD Pack $14.99

34. Barn Dance
00102568 Book/CD Pack $14.99

35. Lindsey Stirling
00109715 Book/CD Pack $19.99

36. Hot Jazz
00110373 Book/CD Pack $14.99

37. Taylor Swift
00116361 Book/CD Pack $14.99

38. John Williams
00116367 Book/CD Pack $14.99

39. Italian Songs
00116368 Book/CD Pack $14.99

41. Johann Strauss
00121041 Book/CD Pack $14.99

42. Light Classics
00121935 Book/Online Audio $14.99

43. Light Orchestra Pop
00122126 Book/Online Audio $14.99

44. French Songs
00122123 Book/Online Audio $14.99

45. Lindsey Stirling Hits
00123128 Book/Online Audio $19.99

47. Light Masterworks
00124149 Book/Online Audio $14.99

48. Frozen
00126478 Book/Online Audio $14.99

50. Songs For Beginners
00131417 Book/Online Audio $14.99

Disney characters and artwork © Disney Enterprises, Inc.
Prices, contents, and availability
subject to change without notice.

7777 W. BLUEMOUND RD. P.O. BOX 13819 MILWAUKEE, WI 53213

www.halleonard.com

1014